I believe that every worker has the

RIGHT
TO
EXPECT
FAIRNESS
IN REGARD TO ALL ASPECTS OF
HIS/HER
JOB

BUT LIKE ALL FREEDOMS, THIS RIGHT HAS
TO BE FOUGHT FOR AND VIGOROUSLY
GUARDED.

FORMATTED
FOR
EASE OF READING

A publication of Western Star Publishing LLC
All rights reserved
3nd Edition 2000

Contents

Dear Worker:

I believe a Bad Boss can make you sick. I believe a dangerous workplace can kill you. I've seen it happen. Maybe you have, too.

I've been a worker all my life, holding down everything from day laboring jobs to managing a million dollar company. I've also had more than my share of the worst bosses and jobs I think exist on this planet. Once I almost lost my sight because I was afraid to complain to an abusive boss about my unsafe workplace. I learned the hard way to fight back. You don't have to.

Most of the job abuses listed in this book I personally experienced. The suggestions I make are the things I did and do to fight back. They worked for me.

It's a jungle out there in the world of work today, and the rules seem to change daily. And as much as I hope this book helps you, I make no claims nor accept any responsibility for any actions you may decide to take as the result of reading this book.

BUT CONSIDER THIS!   If you are suffering from a bad boss or job, and you do nothing, things will probably change.

THEY'LL PROBABLY CHANGE FOR THE WORSE. WHY JUST SIT THERE AND TAKE IT?

Forward

Why a book about bad jobs and bosses?
There are many reasons. There are hundreds of
books and guides dispensing advise for the boss and
employer in dealing with problem employees and
workers. But there are few books and guides
offering help for the rank and file worker in dealing
with abusive bosses and companies. It's time to
level the playing field a little. Today, bosses and
employers wield most of the power, and this places
the worker at a disadvantage. Workers today often
face increased workloads for the same or less pay.
Employers often lie to the workers, and often
disregard worker safety. In some industries,
workers are regarded as little more than disposable
inventory.

7

Have you ever noticed the double standard that seems to exist between corporations, their executives, and the rank and file worker?

...The worker who moves from job to job to make more money or better his lot is considered a job jumper and not reliable. But the CEO and upper level managers who move from job to job to make more money or better their lot are considered merely workers making career moves or advancing in their professions.

...The CEO and upper level managers who do a good job and make money for the company are rewarded with fat bonuses and other perks. But the worker who works hard and makes money for the company is honored by being made "employee of the month." Being made "employee of the month"

8

may make you feel good, but it won't pay for your health care insurance, help send your children to college or trade school, or put food on your table. Your company may try to tell you that the "employee of the month program" is good for morale. What it is good for is the company's pocketbook. What does it cost them to make you "employee of the month?" If the "employee of the month program" is such a coveted prize, ask yourself why the CEO and the upper level managers don't vie for such a plum?

...The company keeps records of your work performance, to include their assessment of you, and claims it as its right. But often those very companies frown on your keeping records of their performance, and or mistreatment.

...Companies and bosses can belong to any organization that helps them negotiate in their interests with the workers. But more often than not, those very companies vigorously oppose any attempt by the workers to organize a union to help them negotiate in their best interests.

...Companies that can provide jobs and executives with certain skills, are often lured into communities with offers of tax breaks, financial grants, moving expenses, etc. But workers who will make the machinery of the company turn are most often offered nothing, and must pay their relocation expenses.

These double standards are unfair. They keep the worker in a perpetual state of servitude. Often the only way out is to become part of the

10

management team, which often means joining the side of the exploiters.

It is not my purpose to deplore the double standard and abuse that is so much a part of the workplace today. But it is important to understand that this double standard creates a society in which some classes of people are perceived more equal than others, where some are regarded as less capable than others, where some are thought less deserving than others.

How many times have you heard someone say, only the most talented and intelligent rise to the top. If that's true, explain why so many of the inventions and innovations come from the rank and file workers. Maybe the truth is that it is the most ruthless and talented exploiters of people who rise

11

to the top. It has been said that to be a good manager, one must be ruthless, and that a failed manager wasn't ruthless enough. Often the inequity and unfairness is justified as one group being more capable and deserving than another. But most often it is simply a way to justify exploitation. Those who must work twelve to fifteen hours a day to make ends meet can not afford to better their lot or get a good education, much less find the time. And yet many of these people are viewed as less capable than those whose circumstances enable them to escape grinding exploitation.

The supporters of this double standard often justify the status quo with false arguments and lies, and worse still, convince some of us to accept them.

For an example, who now would believe that slavery was God's will? Yet during the time of slavery in this country, there were defenders who alleged slavery was God's will, and there where those who believed it. Today there are captains of giant corporations who allege that they are the machinery that drives the world, feeds the world, and brings to the world the highest standard of living the world has ever seen. And there are many who believe them. But when you look around at the pollution, the wanton exploitation of the earth's resources, the poverty, you have to ask, are these corporations really serving us and the common good, or are they really serving their own interests without regard to the consequences.

This double standard and exploitation of the

worker has resulted in a lower regard for the rank and file worker, and an appalling disregard for their feelings and rights. Consider, in some companies it's now common practice to spy on employees. There was a time when privacy was considered the right of everyone, but no more. There are cases where employees have been blacklisted. Much of the work done by rank and file workers is little valued today. If it were, why do so many companies move their operations to foreign lands for cheap labor? Cheap does not equate with something that is valued. Finally, ask workers who have been the victims of company mergers what consideration for their feelings and rights they received.

How, then, is employer exploitation and

abuse confronted and defeated?

One way is to keep records and publicize it. Many will agree it was the novel, "Uncle Tom's Cabin" that had a major influence in defeating slavery. It was the horror stories of child labor in this country that helped bring about the cry for reform.

Closer to home, how can you stand up to the company and boss who may be abusing you? Much the same way. And that's what much of this book is about: keeping records of abuse, and using those records to seek relief and justice. This book has been called the "write up book." That's what much of this book will be advocating: writing up your bad boss and company.

Why?

Because your company writes up those employees they consider problems, and who they may have to deal with in a more formal way in the future. It helps them win in litigation against the worker.

Just as the company has the right to keep records on you, you have the right to keep records on them. Failing to exercise this right with an abusive company can cost your plenty.

The approach outlined in this book is only one way to stand up to employer abuse. It may not resolve your problem or work for you. However, keeping written records of abuse and using them effectively, has helped others to obtain justice and fair treatment.

Wishing you justice and fair treatment in your workplace.

THE WHYS AND WHEREFORES

What makes a job bad?

There can be many things that make a good job bad, but the two major factors are: The type of work the job requires,and the people who supervise and work with you on the job.

There is not much you can do about the type of work the job requires, if you don't like it. Sorry about that. But there are things you can do about your job, if the people who are a part of your job are making your life miserable. The primary focus of this book will be about those people and companies who make good jobs, bad jobs, and what you can do about it.

First, how do you know if you're in a bad job? Dumb question, you say. Anyone can tell if they're in a bad job. Well, not always.

Many people blame themselves for their problems on the job, even if their problems are not their fault. Then there are some people who believe the company is always right, even if the company is being abusive. And there are some people who believe that suffering humiliation, unfair treatment, and all other job abuses are things that must be endured if one wishes to keep his or her job. Thank goodness everyone doesn't feel that way, or we'd all still be working 18 hour days in dangerous sweatshops.

So, how do you know if you're in a bad job?

<u>You know you're in a bad job if:</u>

➣you begin to feel job stress two hours

before it's time to go to work.

➣there is favoritism at work.

➣you must be on constant guard to watch

your backside.

➣you can't wait for the workday to end.

➣your co-workers act more like enemies

than friends.

➣you've been counting the days until your

retirement, and it's still decades

away.

➣you seemed to have aged ten years in the

last six months.

Seriously, if your job makes you feel just

plain bad, you probably have a bad job.

GOOD JOB STRESS \ BAD JOB STRESS

I'm going to say this more than once because I sincerely believe that bad job stress can be extremely harmful to your health. A BAD JOB CAN MAKE YOU SICK!

There is good stress and bad stress, in life and on the job. Good job stress can be the result of going the extra mile for that good boss and company. Good job stress can be the result of accepting a challenging assignment, that once completed, will benefit you and your boss. Good job stress might be the result of just plain hard work that contributed to your growth and development.

Bad job stress can be caused by bad bosses who treat employees unfairly. They may do such things as play one employee against the other, spy

22

on employees, humiliate employees, and demand

more work than is possible to do.   Bad job stress

can be caused by crummy co-workers who bully

you, backstab, gossip behind your back, and blame

you for their mistakes, etc.

There are other causes of bad job stress

which I will cover in other sections of this book, but

I believe that if the two causes just mentioned were

eliminated, the world of work would change for the

better overnight.

HOW GOOD JOBS AND BOSSES BECOME

BAD JOBS AND BOSSES

I remember the best job I ever had. It was a

joy to get up in the morning and go to work.

The work wasn't all that interesting, and at times it

could be dull. But the atmosphere was a happy

23

one. Our boss was committed to fair play in the workplace. He was truly interested in us and our success on the job. Yes, he had rules and standards that we were expected to follow, and we did, willingly. He stood up for us, and we stood up for him and the company. I was convinced that there wasn't a problem that could arise in the workplace that we couldn't solve.

How did this boss get to be so good? He had a good attitude, and he took the job of being a good boss seriously. He had high standards, and he made us feel proud to be a part of his department.

Then our good boss was transferred, and a new boss was assigned to our department.

The new boss had very different ideas about fair treatment. The rules and standards remained

24

the same, but they could now be easily broken,

especially if you were among the new boss's pets.

Some of the boss's pets became company spies, and

co-workers who had once been friends, became our

enemies. Fights broke out among employees, and

there were unfair dismissals. Production and the

quality of work declined, and the new boss blamed

it on the employees, and took away some of our

privileges as punishment. Absenteeism became

rampant, and those of us who did come in to work

had to work twice as hard to make up for those who

were missing. Some of us were reprimanded for not

being able to keep up. That's when I quit.

How do good bosses and jobs go bad? A

change in management.

There is another reason why good bosses and jobs become bad. They go bad because of the flaws and undesirable aspects of human nature.

Let's face it. There are those among us whose nature is such that they will get away with what they are allowed to get away with. That is one of the reasons we have laws. There are those who will lie, cheat, use people in unmerciful ways, even keep slaves if it were allowed. There is no reason to not believe that such people exist in the workplace, and in positions of managers, bosses, and owners of companies, large and small. And when there are such persons in positions of authority in the workplace, you have the danger of your good job becoming a bad job.

Companies and Bosses who intend to take advantage of their workers will test the waters first. An example might be that your boss suddenly announces that all employees will have to work on Saturday, when there is a need.

If the employees accept the order without question, the message the boss and company receive is that of employee acceptance. The company and boss will quickly come to expect compliance and will have little reservation about ordering a Sunday work rule, when they determine a need for it. It won't matter to them that your weekend now belongs to the company. Why should they care if you have to sit by the phone, waiting for their call. After all, you didn't seem to care when the order was made.

Doing nothing when the boss or company tries to force concessions on you, is a mistake. It is a mistake because by doing nothing, you are letting the company get concessions for free. The profit from getting concessions from you is 100%. Nice deal, huh? For them, but what about you?

Now let's take the same situation and consider it from another approach. The company announces that on a specific date employees will be required to work Saturdays, when there is a need.

But now instead of meekly accepting the order, you or a group of employees raise some questions and concerns: Will there be overtime? Is there any recourse if working Saturdays results in a hardship, such as no child care available. Will the company be willing to work out some

28

accommodations so employees can have planned weekends off?

What kind of message does the boss and company get now? Some might say that the message is that the employees are being uncooperative and insensitive, but you and I know that that's nonsense. The message the boss and company gets is that their employees have lives, too. And even though the employees are not opposed to working Saturday, they would like some assurances and concessions from the company concerning their welfare. Why should the employees bear the entire cost of the concessions?

There is now a cost to the company and boss for the concessions-a justified cost. The company and the boss will factor in this cost when they

29

attempt to force further concessions on the

employees.

GOOD BOSSES AND COMPANIES CONSIDER

THEIR EMPLOYEES WHEN THERE IS A NEED

TO MAKE CONCESSIONS, AND SHARE THE

COST OF THE CONCESSIONS.

SOME SIGNS OF A GOOD COMPANY AND

BOSS

➤low employee turnover

➤the boss the employee is to work for takes

part in the interview

➤the atmosphere is open and pleasant

➤favorable comments from current and former

employees

➤the interview makes you feel good

SOME SIGNS OF A BAD COMPANY AND BOSS

➤high employee turnover

➤the atmosphere appears to be closed and tense

➤the interview makes you feel like you've been

processed

➤negative comments from current and former

employees

A FEW WORDS TO GOOD BOSSES AND COMPANIES

If you are a good boss or company owner

who is reading this book, please know that you are

valued and appreciated, not only by those who are

fortunate to have you, but by the legions who wish

they did. However, you may be a good boss who

31

has a bad boss who makes it almost impossible for you to be a good boss. If this is the case, please know that you have the understanding and respect of many, and that you may find the practical approaches section of this book helpful in fighting back. Good luck to you.

WHY FIGHT BACK? WHY NOT JUST QUIT?

In many parts of the county jobs are hard to come by. Why not at least try to make your abusive job tolerable?

Maybe you've been on the job long enough to have earned benefits that would take years to earn by starting over on another job.

32

Maybe you just don't want to be pushed out because of abuse.

Maybe you believe the fight for justice in the workplace is a worthwhile fight, not only for you, but for your children.

Bad Bosses, Bad Jobs, Fight Back!!

Section 1

For the Record

The write up

FOR THE RECORD

WRITING UP YOUR BAD BOSS AND HIS

COMPANY

You might be asking, isn't this what the boss
and the company do to discipline and fire workers?
<u>YOU BET THEY DO!</u> This is formal discipline,
also called documentation. The boss and the
company have a right to do this, and it can be a
good thing for both the company and the workers.

But the problem with this type of formal
discipline comes when you have an abusive boss or
company. <u>THEN THE WRITE UP YOU GET
CAN BE ONE SIDED, AND UNFAIRLY USED
AGAINST YOU. IT CAN EVEN AFFECT YOUR
FUTURE.</u>

37

Bosses and companies use the WRITE UP because they know that a written record is a powerful tool that can be used to: FIRE YOU, DENY YOU PROMOTIONS AND BENEFITS, CONTROL YOU, AND THREATEN YOUR FUTURE. And companies spend thousands of dollars teaching their bosses how to use the written record in their best interests.

If your company hasn't gotten around to teaching you how to use the written record in your best interests, don't hold your breath waiting for them to show you how.

In the following pages I will show you one way you can use the written record in your interest

38

when you find yourself in an abusive workplace.

REMEMBER: ALWAYS KEEP THE ORIGINAL

COPY OF ANY WRITE UPS YOU DO.

HERE'S A QUICK, EASY, AND SIMPLE WAY

TO MAKE A RECORD.

THE WRITE UP

Let's say your boss chews you out in front of your co-workers or customers. <u>THAT'S ABUSE!</u> Well, isn't it? You can lick your wounds and forget it, or you can start a record of the abuse you're enduring, and maybe even haul you boss into court and make him pay.

<u>HERE'S ONE WAY:</u>

THE BASIC THREE OF THE WRITE UP

1.   Do the write up in private (even in the

bathroom if there is no other place), and as soon

after the abuse occurs as possible.

2.   Write it up in this order:

DATE-TIME-LOCATION, and then what

happened. DO NOT EXAGGERATE (your

honesty will make your write up more credible, and

make it more difficult for your boss or company to

discredit you.)

3.   Keep your WRITE UP at home, in a folder,

and in a safe place.

THIS WHOLE PROCESS TAKES ONLY

MINUTES, BUT CAN PAY YOU UNTOLD

BENEFITS. AND THIS WRITE UP CAN BE USED

FOR MOST SITUATIONS.

WHY BOTHER DOING THE WRITE UP?

***   It may put a stop to the abuse. (I'll

explain how later)

***   Your <u>WRITE UPS</u> can help counter

untruthful records the company may

be keeping on you. <u>And don't think</u>

<u>this doesn't happen!</u>

***   You'll have a written record of the

abuse inflicted on you that you can use

in court or litigation.

43

***   Abusive bosses and companies tend to

get worse before they get better, and

you may need all the protection you

can get. Your written record can be a

powerful tool, if your problems with

your company end up in court.

<u>WRITE UPS CAN BE POWERFUL ENOUGH TO

MAKE YOU THE WINNER AND YOUR

COMPANY THE LOSER.</u>

SECTION 2

BAD BOSSES

Bad Bosses, Bad Jobs, Fight Back!!

BOSSES

Good bosses have hundreds of positive qualities.

The fundamentals of any good boss are: <u>A commitment to fairness in all aspects of the workplace, and respectful treatment.</u>

<u>BAD BOSSES</u>

*use you for their own gain,

*look out for themselves first,

*blame you for their mistakes,

*spy on you,

*have favorites - at your expense,

*make you feel sick,

AND MAKE YOUR LIFE A LIVING HELL

ATILLA

ATTILA

The boss who insults you (chews you out) in front of your co-workers, customers or other people.

This is humiliating and embarrassing, and it can cause you to lose the respect of your co-workers.

Worse still, if you do nothing about it, you will likely become the whipping boy or girl who gets blamed every time anything goes wrong. Your life can become a living hell.

IF ATTILA HAS TARGETED YOU, DON'T DESPAIR. READ ON!

49

***   When Attila insults you in front of others, write him up. The date, time, place, and what happened.

***   Go to Attila and tell him/her how he embarrassed you and ask him to stop.

***   Write up your meeting with Attila, including how Attila responded to you, even if he/she didn't respond.

***   Continue this procedure three times if Attila doesn't stop, then make copies of your write ups and go to Attila's boss and ask for help.

***   If you get no help from the

company, seek outside help. (see section 7)

REMEMBER: ALWAYS KEEP THE ORIGINAL

COPY OF ANY WRITE UPS YOU DO.

What this action might accomplish:

Attila may have been in trouble over his behavior in the past, and your actions will make him stop for his own good.

Your write ups will establish a pattern of abuse that can be a powerful tool you can use in litigation or court.

If Attila fires you for complaining, you can use your write ups to show abuse and unfair treatment.

REMEMBER: ATTILA CARES FOR NO ONE BUT HIMSELF. HE WILL CONSIDER YOUR FEELINGS ONLY IF IT IS IN HIS INTEREST.

REMEMBER: ALWAYS KEEP THE ORIGINAL

COPY OF ALL YOUR WRITE UPS.

THE BUTT COVER

THE BUTT COVER

The boss who just can't remember, or denies

that he told you to do something, especially when

that something he told you to do resulted in trouble.

(the boss tells you to stack company valuables in a

place where they get stolen, then says he didn't tell

you to put them there)

THERE ARE THOUSANDS OF BUTT COVER BOSSES. YOU COULD COVER THE INTERSTATE WITH THEM.

If you let the Butt Cover get away with it,

you will risk becoming the whipping boy or girl at

work who gets blamed for everything that goes

wrong. If you leave the Butt Cover unchecked, you could lose your job. FIGHT BACK!

***   Write up the incident - date, time,

place, what happened.

***   Tell him/her you were blamed

unfairly.

***   Send a copy of your Write Up to the

Butt Cover's boss, asking for a

resolution.

What this action might accomplish:

The Butt Cover may be in trouble for this already and will stop using you.

The Butt Cover's boss may act to stop the abuse.

Your Write Ups will help you show a pattern of abuse that you can use effectively in litigation.

It will send a message you will not tolerate such abuse.

THE SNIPER

THE SNIPER

When things go wrong at work, the Sniper blames the first convenient employee he/she can find.

THE SNIPER IS ALSO KNOWN AS THE FINGER POINTER. YOU AND I BOTH KNOW WHERE HE CAN STICK HIS FINGER.

If you let the Sniper get off by shooting the blame at you, your job will be in jeopardy, and your chance for promotion will be cut off.

SHOOT BACK

*** If the Sniper tries to write you up, (discipline you) refuse to sign the

write up on the grounds it is unfair.
Do your own write up of the Sniper,
and send a copy to the Sniper's Boss,
asking for help.

***   Go to the Sniper and tell him/her that
he blamed you unfairly. Write up
his/her response, even if the Sniper
doesn't respond.

***   If the Sniper continues to blame you
unfairly, write it up, and go to the
Sniper's Boss in person and ask for
help.

What this action might accomplish:

You will have a record of abuse established that can be used against the Sniper in litigation.

It may put a stop to the finger pointing.

It may bring the Sniper's Boss into the problem. The Sniper's Boss may side with the Sniper, but he may side with you and resolve the problem.

It can help to more clearly define your job responsibility for you, which will go a long way in keeping the Sniper from using you when he's in trouble again.

REMEMBER:

IT DOES ABSOLUTELY NO GOOD TO TRY TO

GET ON THE GOOD SIDE OF THE SNIPER TO

KEEP HIM FROM POINTING HIS FINGER AT

YOU. WHEN THE SNIPER IS IN TROUBLE, HE

HAS NO FRIENDS, ONLY PEOPLE TO BLAME.

REMEMBER: ALWAYS KEEP THE ORIGINAL

COPY OF ALL YOUR WRITE UPS

THE PET KEEPER

THE PET KEEPER

The Boss who favors other employees at your expense. (you have to work extra weekends so the boss's pet can have off. Or the boss punishes you for being late, but fails to punish his favorite, who is always late.)

PET KEEPERS SHOULDN'T BE BOSSES. THEY SHOULD WORK IN ZOOS, OR BETTER YET, BE IN ONE OF THE CAGES.

The Pet Keeper boss often uses his pet as a spy. If you do nothing, you will be given all the bad assignments, and face harassment from the boss's pet.

TURN UP THE HEAT

***   Look in the company handbook to see

if the boss is breaking company rules

by giving his pet favored treatment.

Chances are he is (his pet comes in late but

isn't disciplined)

***   Write up each incident you see where

the boss is breaking company rules

with his pet. When you have three,

preferably five (it won't take long)

make copies and send them to the Pet

Keeper's Boss. Date the copies you

send. This will insure a quick

response. You do not have to

sign your name.

What this action might accomplish:

Make the Pet Keeper's Boss aware of trouble in the

department.

It may resolve the problem.

Put pressure on the Pet Keeper to curb his behavior.

You will have a record if you decide to bring

litigation for discrimination or harassment.

THE LIAR WITH A PEN

THE LIAR WITH A PEN

The boss who disciplines you (writes you up) for

something you didn't do.

This is the kind of boss who believes he can make

his lies about you true by putting them in writing -

AND HE WILL IF YOU DO NOTHING.

DO NOT ACCEPT THE LIE

***   The Liar will ask you to sign his write up of

you. When he does, ask if you may write a

comment on the write up before you sign. If

he agrees, write these words: I protest this

discipline as unfair and unfounded. Ask for

a copy of the write up. This is your right.

Then mail a copy of the write up to the
Liar's boss, asking for help.

***   If the Liar refuses to let you write a
comment on the write up, refuse to sign.
Then in privacy do your own write up, to
include why the discipline is unfair.

***   Mail a copy of your write up to your boss's
boss, and on a separate sheet of paper ask
that the discipline be removed from your
record.

***   If there is no response from the Liar's boss
within ten days, seek outside help. (see
section 7)

What this action might accomplish:

It may clear your record.

It can challenge your boss to support his accusations with facts.

Your Write Up will be a most useful document in litigation with the company.

THE LIAR WITH A BIGGER PEN

THE LIAR WITH A BIGGER PEN

The boss who gives you an unfair job evaluation

This boss thinks he can harass you, even push you out of the company by giving you a bad job review. YOU CAN BE DISCREDITED AND HAVE YOUR FUTURE THREATENED IF YOU DO NOTHING.

STOP THE LIAR

***   Refuse to sign the evaluation

***   Ask for a copy. <u>This is your right!!</u>

***   Write up the incident and send a copy to the

Liar's boss, asking for help. Ask for another

evaluation.

***   If you get no help from the company, seek

outside help. (see section 7)

What this action might accomplish:

It can establish a record of possible harassment. (untrue things alleged about you in writing can be considered harassment and slander)

Put pressure on your boss to reconsider his evaluation of you.

Clear your record.

REMEMBER: ALWAYS KEEP THE ORIGINAL COPY OF ALL YOUR WRITE UPS.

THE FRINGE BENEFIT SEEKER

THE FRINGE BENEFIT SEEKER

The boss who makes sexual advances - touches you

inappropriately - threatens your job if you refuse

sex.

Whether you're male or female, write it up -

immediately - accurately! (NOTE) males are subject

to sexual harassment, also, and should not fail to

report it.

TAKE ACTION IMMEDIATELY!

*** Go to your boss, and in private tell him/her

that his/her behavior is making you

uncomfortable. (be specific) Ask him/her

to please stop.

77

***   After your meeting with your boss, write up what happened in the meeting, to include your boss's response, even if he didn't respond.

***   Wait for the behavior to stop.

***   If the harassing behavior continues, write it up, and then make copies of all your write ups concerning this behavior and mail them to the president or general manager, asking for help.

***   If there is no response within ten days, seek outside help. (see section 7)

What this action might accomplish:

Stop the harassment.

Arm you with a written record to take the harasser

to court for damages.

THE TURNCOAT

THE TURNCOAT

The boss who is out to please everybody, but will not stand behind you if it would reflect badly on him.

THE TURNCOAT MAY WEAR MANY COATS, BUT THE LINING IN ALL OF THEM IS YELLOW.

The turncoat boss will be all for you and any new ideas you may have to improve the job or workplace. He will even take credit if all goes well. But if all doesn't go well, he will quickly back away from you.

IF YOUR BOSS IS A TURNCOAT:

81

***   Avoid him whenever possible

***   If you need his approval to do something
          new, ask for him to put it in writing. (give
          you written approval) Chances are he won't
          do this.

***   Seek written approval for your new project
          from a boss at a higher level. (go over his
          head)

***   If the turncoat boss gets angry because you
          went to a higher boss for support, tell him
          you needed support for your new project
          that you could count on.

What this action might accomplish:

Lets the turncoat know you expect support or you will seek it elsewhere.

Lets the turncoat's boss know who is really making the contributions to the company.

(NOTE)   The turncoat boss tends to take credit for the good and flees from anything that might reflect badly on him. That's why he is reluctant to put anything in writing.

THE SLAVE DRIVER

THE SLAVE DRIVER
(ALSO KNOWN AS THE PILE DRIVER)

The boss who pours more and more work on you when you are already doing all you can.

THE SLAVE DRIVER SHOULD BE ON THE RECEIVING END OF A PILE DRIVER.

If you try to please the Slave Driver by doing all the extra work he shoves at you, you will quickly be overwhelmed. You will not be able to perform any part of your job well, and will be in danger of losing your job. Your chances of promotion will be diminished.

The Slave Driver usually doesn't listen, so telling him how overworked you are and asking for relief won't help. <u>The Slave Driver has to be shown.</u>

***   Make a work study.

***   Get a legal pad, and during your work day, write down all the jobs you do and the time it takes to do them. This may sound difficult, but it is easy. (examples) 9am typed letter - answered 6 phone calls, wrote messages 9:25am - 9:26am began filing etc. At the end of your working day add up the time. List all things you didn't get done or have time to get done. Do this for three working days. (NOTE)   If your work doesn't permit you to carry a legal pad, carry

a small pocket book to use and then transfer
it to a legal pad.

*** Make an appointment with your boss and
take copies of your work study with you.
Tell the Slave Driver you're concerned about
not being able to do your job well because
of too much work and not enough day.
Hand him the reports. Ask for his help.

*** After the meeting with the Slave Driver,
write it up, date, time, place and what
happened. Write up the slave driver's
response to your request for help, even if he
doesn't respond.

(NOTE)   You will need the write up and the

records of your work activity (your work study) if

the slave driver continues to abuse you)

***   If the Slave Driver continues to pile the

        work on you, make copies of your write up

        and work studies and mail them to the Slave

        Driver's boss, asking for help.

***   If no one in the company will help you, seek

        outside help. (see section 7)

What this action might accomplish:

Possibly stop the abuse.

You may get a review of your job duties and a lighter work load.

You may get a raise.

Establish a record of possible abuse and your efforts to stop it. This can be used in litigation.

(NOTE)   I once did this and got a raise in pay and a lighter work load.

THE PINK SLIPPER

THE PINK SLIPPER

The boss who is in danger of losing his/her job.

This boss may or may not be a bad boss, but what you do can affect your future with the company.

***   If this boss is a good boss and does not deserve to be fired, do whatever you can on your job to make the boss look good. (good jobs are hard to come by, but good bosses are even harder to come by)

***   If this boss is a bad boss and deserves to be fired, don't do anything visible or out of the ordinary to get this boss fired. This type of behavior will only reflect badly on you, and

91

may put you in a bad light with the new

incoming boss.

*** Instead:

1. Concentrate and focus on your work.

2. Keep busy so there's little time to talk to

   your bad boss.

3. Avoid discussing your bad boss in a

   negative or positive way with your

   co-workers.

4. Keep alert to any danger signs in the

   workplace that might affect you.

What this action might accomplish:

Keep you from getting involved in a controversy that may work against you.

Helps you to create an image that you are a loyal worker.

May help your good boss keep his/her job.

Help you get off to a good start with the new incoming boss.

Bad Bosses, Bad Jobs, Fight Back!!

SECTION 3

CRUMMY

CO-WORKERS

CO-WORKERS:

are those you work with

who do the same type of work

are considered your equals.

CO-WORKERS WHO ARE:

BULLIES, TATTLETALES, LOW

BALLERS, GOSSIP MONGERS,

BOSS'S SPIES, AND LAZY FOOT

DRAGGERS ARE:

CRUMMY CO-WORKERS!

REMEMBER: ALWAYS KEEP THE ORIGINAL

COPY OF ALL YOUR WRITE UPS.

THE BULLY

THE BULLY

The co-worker who picks on you - criticizes you -
pushes you around - humiliates you.

Most every workplace has a bully or potential one.
If you let the bully, bully you, you will lose the
respect of your co-workers. If you do nothing about
the bully, his abuse of you will get worse to the
point where you will either quit or do something
that might get you fired.

Remember:

The Bully will only stop picking on you
when it is in his best interest to stop.

***   Write Up every time the Bully picks on you.

(write it up immediately)

***   Report the Bully's abuse of you to your boss

with copies of your Write Ups. (this will

often put an end to the abuse)

***   If your boss doesn't respond to your

complaints, go to your boss's boss and ask

for help. Do a Write Up of your request for

help, and the response you got.

***   If all fails within the company, seek outside

help. (see section 7)

What this action might accomplish:

Establish a record of abuse that you can use in litigation.

Put a stop to the abuse.

Keep you from being seen as a easy target in the workplace.

REMEMBER: ALWAYS KEEP THE ORIGINAL COPY OF ALL YOUR WRITE UPS.

THE HIBERNATOR

THE HIBERNATOR

The lazy co-worker who only does his/her share of work when the boss is looking. You end up carrying his/her load.

WAKE UP THE HIBERNATOR!!

***   Get real busy on your job so there is no time to help do the Hibernator's work. (it will pile up quick and someone will notice)

***   Avoid the Hibernator in the lunchroom and on break times so you will not become identified with him/her.

***   If it is appropriate, ask for a transfer.

(NOTE)   If the Hibernator happens to be the boss's pet, refer to the section on bad bosses, "THE PET KEEPER" for suggestions on what to do.

What this action might accomplish:

Send a message to the Hibernator that you will not do both your work and part or all of his work.

It will distance you from the Hibernator so you are not identified with him or her.

It will focus on the Hibernator's undone work and make him more accountable.

REMEMBER: ALWAYS KEEP THE ORIGINAL

COPY OF ALL YOUR WRITE UPS.

THE 00 SPY

THE 00 SPY

The co-worker who thinks he can get favorite treatment from the boss by spying for him.

Company spies are usually easy to detect. They can be the boss's pet or the person who seems a little to interested in you and how you feel about your job and the boss. It can be that person who seems to have other interests at work besides doing his job.

When there is a spy or spies in the workplace, it is a sign that there is distrust by management of the rank and file workers. Also, the boss may be looking for someone to blame his problems on. Don't let it be you.

WHAT YOU CAN DO.

*** Offer nothing to anyone in the way of good or bad opinions about the company or the boss. (it's difficult to find fault with no opinion)

*** Concentrate on your job.

*** Don't be seen at work at non work times unless there is a good reason.

What this action might accomplish:

Keep the spy from targeting you.

Keep you from becoming a scapegoat or seen as a collaborator by your co-workers.

If you want to expose and discredit the company spy:

Tell him that you heard something that will affect the company. (tell him you were called and asked to come to an organizational meeting in a downtown cafe.)

If he is the spy, he will tell his boss and some type of action will be taken. You will then know who the spy is, and when there is no meeting, the spy will lose credibility.

REMEMBER: ALWAYS KEEP THE ORIGINAL
COPY OF ALL YOUR WRITE UPS.

THE LOW BALLER

THE LOW BALLER
(Also known as the back stabber)

The co-worker who tries to look good by making you look bad. (he/she calls attention to any mistake you make)

FIGHT BACK

***   Call attention to his/her mistakes.

***   Find something at work that you can do better than the low baller and challenge her to a friendly competition - in front of the boss if possible.

***   Find something about the Low Baller to

113

complain about (he leaves his tools all over -

her perfume leaves a trail)

<u>Remember:</u>

<u>The Low Baller will keep using you if there</u>

<u>is no cost to him or her.</u>

What this action might accomplish:

It will put the Low Baller on the defensive and take time from her that she used to use to low ball you.

Your actions of fighting back may make the Low Baller wary of you and she will look around for someone else to low ball.

THE GOSSIP MONGER

THE GOSSIP MONGER

The co-worker who spreads gossip or makes up rumors about you. (your husband left you - your child flunked out of school - etc.)

IF THE GOSSIP MONGER HAS TARGETED YOU, <u>STRIKE BACK</u>

***   Go to the gossip monger (they are usually well known) and tell him/her that you just over heard a rumor, but you wanted to check with him/her before spreading it around. Then tell him/her the gossip she/he has been spreading about you, but make him/her the subject of it. (I heard your child flunked out of school. Then look him/her

straight in the eye and walk away.)

What this action might accomplish:

Send a strong message that you are on to him/her.

Lets the Gossip Monger know that you will retaliate.

Encourages the Gossip Monger to stop or target someone else.

REMEMBER: ALWAYS KEEP THE ORIGINAL COPY OF ALL YOUR WRITE UPS.

SECTION 4

UNSAFE WORKING

CONDITIONS

UNSAFE WORKING CONDITIONS

It is in the best interests of employers to provide safe working conditions, if not for their concern for your welfare, then because of the high cost to them if you get hurt. For this reason, you will often find a quick response from your employer when you express a concern for your safety.

You should never hesitate for a moment to report to your employer an unsafe condition at your work. <u>It is your health and welfare that is at stake.</u>

WHEN YOUR EMPLOYER REFUSES TO CORRECT UNSAFE WORKING CONDITIONS:

***   Your first step is to clearly identify the unsafe working condition (a faulty piece of equipment, boxes piled too high so they will fall, computer screen unshielded, etc.)

***   Your second step is to write it up (on the company form, if there is one. If not, do your own) then report the condition to your employer.

If your employer fails to respond or correct the problem:

A: Report the problem to your local OSHA office with a copy of your Write Up. (see section 7)

B: Do whatever you can to protect

yourself from the unsafe working

condition, calling in sick, if you have

to.

REMEMBER: ALWAYS KEEP THE ORIGINAL

COPY OF ALL YOUR WRITE UPS.

SECTION 5

LAYOFFS -

CUTBACKS -

PAYCUTS

LAYOFFS

WHEN YOU ARE NOTIFIED OF A LAYOFF:

*** Go to the highest supervisor or official in the company you can get to see.

*** Take a notebook with you to the meeting and ask the following questions:

1. The exact date of the layoff, and for how long it will be.

2. Is the layoff expected to be permanent.

3.   Is there to be a recall, and if so, ask

to be on the list.

4.   Do you have to reapply for work to

be considered for recall. Some

companies won't tell you unless you

ask and you will risk losing your

recall rights.

5.   Ask for a list of benefits the

employer may be offering the laid

off workers.   (severance pay -

retraining - etc.) Sometimes you are

not told this unless you ask. There

may be a time limit for which you

can qualify for such benefits.

6.   Ask about transfer possibilities

within the company.

***   Go to your employment office and ask for a

list or referral of assistance for laid off

workers.

CUTBACKS

WHEN YOU ARE FACED WITH CUTBACKS
AT WORK.

*** First find out if the proposed cutback is

necessary, or is being done to boost profits

and increase the workload, or other hidden

reasons. To do this, ask as many questions

as you can about the reason why the cutback

is needed. (example) is the company losing

money, are there reduced sales. Go to the

library and ask the librarian for a financial

report on your company. If the reasons for

the cutback seem suspicious, seek outside

help. (see section 7)

If the cutback seems genuine,

***   Try to make your job indispensable.

***   Check to see if other tasks can be done by you, and volunteer to do them.

***   Don't miss any days. (if the company is intent on cutting back, they will use your missed days as an excuse to cut back on your hours)

***   Volunteer for extra duty.

***   Keep a written record of all the extra work you did and how hard it was to do. You can use this record to negotiate with the

company when it becomes more prosperous

again, or to justify a pay adjustment.

PAYCUTS

***   First, find out if the paycut is necessary, or if it is being done to boost profits and increase workload. To do this, ask as many questions as you can about the reasons for the paycut. If they seem suspicious, seek outside help (refer to section 7)

***   If the paycut seems to be a genuine need:

1.   Ask if you will be expected to do the same work for less pay on a permanent basis, or if there will be some type of adjustment.

2.   Ask if you can form a committee to find some cost savings ideas to use in lieu of the paycut.

3.   Ask for extra time off so you can work another part time job to make up for the loss of pay. (example) leave an hour earlier - etc.

If your employer insists on the paycut without making any concessions:

1.   Accept it but request a meeting to discuss the paycut within three months. Put your request in writing and send a copy to your employer. By doing this, you are not accepting

the paycut as final. This will give

you an opportunity to recover your

lost pay if the company's position

improves.

NOTE: Try to avoid signing anything that

might lock you into agreeing to a permanent paycut

or accepting it without the chance to negotiate at a

later date.

SECTION 6

MINIMIZING BAD

WORK REFERENCES

HOW TO MINIMIZE POSSIBLE BAD

WORK REFERENCES

If you are fired and you will need a reference from that employer to help you find another job.

***   On a sheet of paper list the name of the company you were fired from, your dates of employment and your position. Then list some of your positive contributions to the company. (never late, good attendance, willing to do all jobs, etc.)

***   Make some copies and take one to your former employer, the one you were fired from. Ask to see the personnel director or person who does the hiring and firing.

***   At the meeting, explain that you need to list his company as a reference in looking for work. Then hand him the copy you made which lists your contributions. Tell him you would appreciate his agreement when he is called for a reference on you. Tell him you need the reference to secure another job, and that it will benefit no one if you have to go to court to get fair treatment.

WHAT TO TELL A PROSPECTIVE EMPLOYER ABOUT THE COMPANY YOU WERE FIRED

FROM. IT IS ALWAYS BEST TO BE AS
HONEST AS YOU CAN.

***   When asked about the company you were
        fired from, speak highly of the company.
        State that certain circumstances arose which
        made it impossible for you to stay with the
        company. If you are asked to explain
        further, explain and also list the
        contributions you made to the company.

***   On an application, list the company and the
        name of the person you gave your list of
        contributions to as the contact person. List
        the reasons for leaving as termination.

NOTE: You can check to see if the company

you were fired from is bad mouthing you by having

a friend call for a reference on you.

Companies have become wary of bad

mouthing fired employees because of the high cost

of lawsuits. (there are numerous cases of fired

employees suing their former employer for giving

them bad references)

SECTION 7

GETTING HELP

Bad Bosses, Bad Jobs, Fight Back!!

GETTING HELP

Before you decide to seek outside help, determine

what the problem is. This will help you look in the

right places, and help others direct you to the

agency that can best help.

SOME EXAMPLES

***   You are being picked on by your boss or a

co-worker. This can be a harassment or

unfair labor issue. You might start by

calling your local employment office and

asking for the agency which handles

harassment or unfair labor concerns.

(sometimes the agency is listed in the phone

book) If you fail to get help this way you

147

can call law offices in your phone book and explain your problem and ask for a referral.

***   You are being pressured for sex or encountering unwanted sexual advances by a co-worker or boss. This is a sexual harassment or assault issue. In many states there is a sexual assault hot line you can call. You'll find it most often in the phone book. There are also government agencies in some states to help with this issue. There are also attorneys who specialize in these issues. They are listed in the phone book.

***   There is an unsafe condition that exists at your place of work and your company has failed to respond to your concerns. This is a worker safety issue. The first agency to contact is O.S.H.A. This agency is found in your phone book.

***   Your company has told you that you must take a pay and benefit cut, but you have reason to suspect the company's motives. This could be an unfair labor practice. A place to start would be the state agency which addresses unfair labor practices. There are also attorneys who specialize in these issues. They are in the phone book.

Possible helpful agencies.

WORKER SAFETY - O.S.H.A.

HARASSMENT ON THE JOB -

DEPARTMENT OF INDUSTRY AND

LABOR RELATIONS (DILR) (STATE)

- FAIR LABOR STANDARDS (STATE)

UNFAIR PAYCUTS AND LAYOFFS - FAIR

LABOR STANDARDS - DEPARTMENT

OF INDUSTRY AND LABOR

RELATIONS (DILR) (STATE)

Other possible helpful agencies:

Attorney referral services - found in phone

books.

Private agencies - found in phone books.

I wish to express my thanks to you for the purchase

of my book, and I hope it will help you.

GOOD LUCK

If you have had a bad job experience or found a way

to fight back, and wish to share it, please send it to:

Western Star Publishing LLC

P.O. Box 5263

Cheyenne, WY 82003

We may ask permission to use it in an upcoming

book.

Gerald L. Johnson

Bad Bosses, Bad Jobs, Fight Back!!

152